A Naval Institute Book for Young Readers

U.S. Navy Ships
and Coast Guard Cutters

The USS Wisconsin *(BB-64) firing her guns during sea trials.*

A Naval Institute Book for Young Readers

U.S. Navy Ships
and Coast Guard Cutters

Rear Admiral M. D. Van Orden, USN (Ret.)

Naval Institute Press
Annapolis, Maryland

An earlier version of this book was originally published in 1969 by Dodd, Mead & Co. as *The Book of U.S. Navy Ships*.

Library of Congress Cataloging-in-Publication Data

Van Orden, M. D., 1921–
    U.S. Navy ships and Coast Guard cutters / M. D. Van Orden.
        p.   cm.
    Rev. ed. of: The book of United States Navy ships. c 1985.
    Summary: Text and photographs introduce the characteristics and purposes of the various types of ships in the present-day Navy and Coast Guard.
    ISBN 0-87021-212-5
    1. United States. Navy—Juvenile literature. 2. Warships—United States—Juvenile literature. 3. United States. Coast Guard—Juvenile literature. [1. United States. Navy. 2. Warships. 3. Ships.] I. Van Orden, M. D., 1921–   Book of United States Navy Ships. II. Title.
VA58.4.V36   1990
359.8′3—dc20   89-13539
                                                                    CIP

Printed in the United States of America on acid-free paper ∞

10 9 8 7 6 5 4 3 2

First Printing

Unless otherwise noted all photographs are courtesy of the U.S. Navy and the U.S. Coast Guard.
Book design by R. Dawn Sollars

To the competent, vigilant, and patriotic men and women who serve in U.S. Navy ships and U.S. Coast Guard cutters.

CONTENTS

FOREWORD

History has shown that control of the seas is an important factor in the development of a powerful nation. But the seas are available for commerce and communication only through the use of ships. Each ship thus becomes a vital link that extends the reach of a whole nation. The essence of whatever is accomplished at sea results from the skill and dedication of the workers who build ships and of the crews who operate them.

The culture of the sea and ships has come to have meaning in environments far from the world's oceans. The word *shipshape,* for instance, has significance everywhere, and the word *shipmate* has come to symbolize the utmost in friendship and loyalty.

To facilitate the use of the seas by a great nation such as the United States, we need to look to the ships of the Navy and Coast Guard. For those of us privileged to have served in them, they bear a personal relationship to our lives. Even when we view them from afar, these ships of the sea services affect us. We do well to learn more about them.

Admiral Arleigh Burke, USN (Ret.)

PREFACE

The sea services of the United States—Navy and Coast Guard—are members of the five U.S. armed forces, along with the Army, Marine Corps, and Air Force. Today's Navy and Coast Guard are complex organizations, composed of ships, boats, aircraft, men, women, guns, missiles, shore bases, and equipment of all types—but the heart of any maritime service is its ships.

This book is written for young men and women who are interested in ships of the modern Navy and Coast Guard. A knowledge and understanding of the U.S. sea services, their ships, and their operations can help young people in deciding upon future service to the nation.

Navy ships and Coast Guard cutters, all with somewhat different missions, are built to a variety of designs, each tailored to the expected service uses. There may be a number of types, classes, conversions, and modifications of each basic design. Modernization requires changes; consequently, improvements in designs and in installed equipments are made as they become necessary. Major changes are made in order to adapt to new techniques of warfare, to new technological advances, and to new mission assignments. For example, the change from sail to steam; the transition from wooden hulls to steel; the advent of nuclear propulsion systems; the shift from guns to missiles; the introduction of radar, sonar, and modern communications; the need for ice-breaking cutters and high-speed patrol and rescue cutters—all of these have resulted in radical changes in ship designs.

The purpose of this book is to illustrate and explain the most important and most representative types and classes of ships in the United States Navy and cutters in the United States Coast Guard, and to describe some of their characteristics. In addition, it will describe the part each ship and vessel plays as a member of the Navy and Coast Guard teams—the fleets and battle groups of today's Navy, and the services of today's Coast Guard.

Upon these ships and these well-trained teams rest our country's power, prestige, and safety. A strong Navy of capable, modern, well-equipped, well-manned ships can do much to discourage aggression and preserve peace. A strong, versatile Coast Guard can provide the maritime safety, law enforcement, and defense of coasts and harbors so vital to our nation.

Activity on flight deck of USS **Saratoga**

1.
INTRODUCTION

The sea has always offered adventure to those who want to cut their ties with the land and sail for far-off places. From earliest times, we have wondered what lay over the horizon. The most courageous adventurers found ways—hollowed-out logs, bamboo rafts, bundles of buoyant materials—to explore the far reaches of the oceans. Modern ships are descendants of these earlier platforms of exploration, and modern seafarers are descendants of the early adventurers.

Today's ships still call forth this spirit. They offer new and interesting sights, visits to new lands, introductions to new peoples, and the challenge of overcoming the hazards often found at sea. But modern ships are complex machines. Their crews must be skilled in all of the techniques needed for safe and efficient operation of these self-contained communities moving about on the oceans of the world.

Navy women serve ashore and aboard noncombatant ships. Here midshipmen, male and female, practice close order drill.

Warships in particular are specialized in design and operations. Their primary purpose is to protect our country's national interests against all enemies, and to attack enemy forces when required by our country's leaders. They are usually designed to be fast and heavily armed with guns and missiles, and they are armored to prevent damage to ship and crew by enemy attacks. Navy warships and Coast Guard cutters are alike in their ability to protect U.S. interests in both home and foreign waters. Their designs reflect those specialized operations that they perform in service to our nation and its people.

Life at sea is different from that led by most shore-dwelling people. There are the constant activities that take place aboard ship—keeping watch over the ship and crew, exercising constant navigational vigilance to avoid danger, caring for engines that provide propulsion and equipments that provide safety, and conducting the many day-to-day routines required to feed and care for the persons aboard. Shipboard life at sea is a constant, twenty-four-hour-a-day, seven-day-a-week period of activity for ships' crews.

Male and female lookouts on the wing of the bridge of a repair ship.

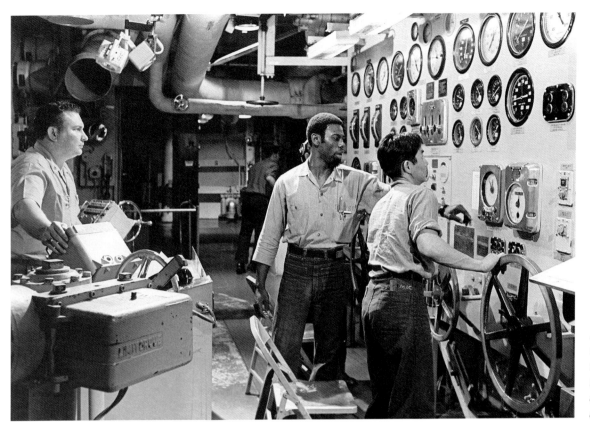

Life at sea—engine-room instruction for a new watch-stander with the chief petty officer overseeing the procedures.

For many years, seagoing life was so difficult that only the strongest, most able men could survive it. Women were not included in ships' crews, most especially not in warships. Today, women have shown that they can serve well in modern ships, performing duties as well as their male counterparts. By law, though, women are not yet permitted to serve aboard U.S. Navy combatant warships. They can, and do, serve aboard auxiliaries and other types that do not normally engage in combat. Coast Guard vessels do not normally engage in combat; therefore, women are assigned as officers and crew members in Coast Guard cutters and boats.

Life at sea—mealtime in the crew's mess aboard the USS Ranger (CV-61).

Among the interesting differences between shipboard life and life ashore are the terms used by seafarers. The terms in common use form almost a different language, with words and phrases that may seem strange but for which there are logical explanations and precedents. The names given to ships, the distinctions between types and classes of ships, the terms that describe ship parts, and especially the shipboard terminology used in orders and commands are all part of this language. These will be explained in the chapters that follow; in later chapters, the individual ships and their classes will be described in detail so that the reader will better understand some of the language of the sea.

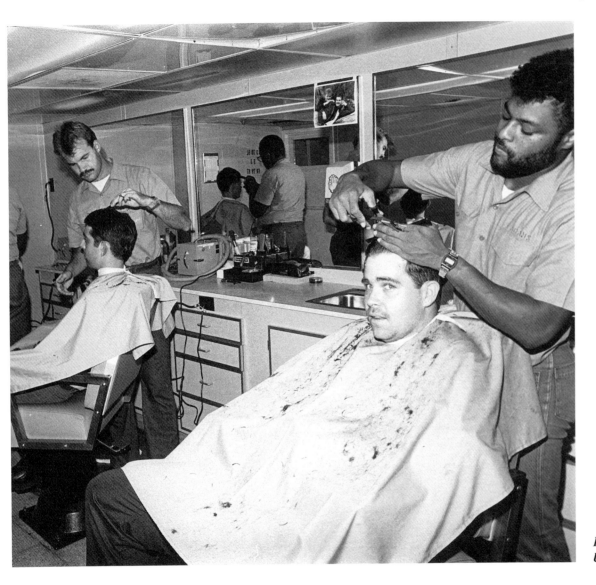

Barbershop aboard the
USS **Ranger**

A starboard view of the USS **Nimitz** *(CVN-68)*

2

SHIP TERMINOLOGY

When those who go to sea talk of their ships, they use words and phrases that may seem strange to others who are not acquainted with the ways of the sea. Yet to seafarers those words and phrases have meanings that are well known and precise. They have been developed over many years by mariners who chose carefully those expressions that would not be misunderstood by other mariners—even during the stress of battle or a raging storm. Many expressions used today are only representative of past traditions of the sea, yet they are cherished and perpetuated by those who are bound together by their common heritage of service at sea.

Ships are always referred to as *she*. There have been many reasons given for this custom. Some think it is because of the beauty a sailor sees in his ship; others say it is because of the difficulty men have in understanding all of "her" different aspects. Perhaps the ancient Greeks started the custom by giving their warships female names to honor Athena, their goddess of war. Whatever the reason, sailors always think and speak of their ship as a *she,* never an *it.*

Mariners always go *on board* a ship, or *in* a ship—never *on* a ship. A favorite saying is, "Seafarers go down to the sea *in* ships; landlubbers go to sea *on* ships."

Don't make the mistake around sailors of calling a ship a boat. A tourist aboard a cruise ship such as the *Queen Elizabeth II* brings forth only disgust among seafarers by saying, "My boat sails at eight o'clock." What is the difference between ships and boats? It is largely a matter of size, with the smaller craft being recognized as boats. A salty old chief petty officer with many years of seagoing experience once stated it simply to a group of midshipmen: "A boat is any craft that can be hoisted aboard a ship—and don't you forget it!" In the Navy there is one exception allowed: submarine sailors call their submarines *boats* despite the fact that by size alone they are classed as ships. Probably this custom dates from the early days, when the subs were known as *pigboats* because of their resemblance in shape and color to young porkers, and because of the way they clustered around their "mother" ships when in harbor. In the Coast Guard it is customary to call all vessels less than 65 feet in overall length *boats;* those greater than 65 feet in length are called *cutters.*

Most people are aware of the use of *port* and *starboard* to mean the left and right sides of a ship or boat, as viewed when facing forward. The *bow* (pronounced to rhyme with cow) is the front part of the ship. It is also sometimes

After deck of the **Ticonderoga,** *showing crew member on the fantail.*

called the *stem*. The *stern* is the ship's tail end. The deck area on the stern is known as the *fantail*—this would be called a back porch if the ship were a house ashore.

Also, many understand that *fore* and *after* are adjectives used to locate shipboard parts or objects; for example, *forecastle* (pronounced foc's'le) and *after deck*. Similarly, *forward* and *aft* indicate toward the bow and toward the stern. Thus, in seagoing language, the bow is the most forward part of a ship, and the stern is the part that is most aft. A fore-and-aft direction is one that runs from the bow to the stern, or stem to stern. The length of a ship is the distance from bow to stern, the width from side to side is called the *beam,* and the *draft* is the vertical distance from the waterline to the deepest part of the hull.

Almost everyone knows that aboard ship the floors are called *decks,* the ceilings are *overheads,* and the walls are known as *bulkheads*. Stairways are always spoken of as *ladders*. When a sailor goes up a ladder to or above the *main deck* (the uppermost deck that extends from bow to stern), he or she will say, "I'm going topside" and when going back down into the ship, "I'm going below." These are the equivalent of upstairs and downstairs to people who are not accustomed to living in ships.

A ship's *superstructure* is that portion of the ship built above the main deck and used for living or working spaces. In an aircraft carrier the superstructure above the

*The **John F. Kennedy** flight deck and island. In an aircraft carrier, the superstructure above the flight deck is called the island.*

Superstructure and bridge wing of a modern destroyer. The bridge of a ship, located in the superstructure, is where the ship is conned by the captain and his officers.

flight deck (that deck used for aircraft landings and takeoffs) is called the *island*. The *bridge* of a ship, located in the superstructure, is the location where the ship is *conned,* or controlled by the captain and the officers.

When a ship is *under way* (floating free—not attached to a land structure such as a pier, and not having an anchor on the bottom), she is driven through the water by *screws,* as the propellers are called. The screws are large, pusher-type propellers that operate underwater at relatively slow speeds—slow, that is, when compared with the puller-type propellers on some airplanes. The screws push the ship through the water at speeds that are measured in

knots. A knot is a measure of speed, not distance. It is a speed of 1 nautical mile per hour. A nautical mile is 6,076 feet (slightly longer than a mile on land) because of its derivation by early navigators from geographic measures—that is, 1 nautical mile was selected as the distance covered by 1 minute ($1/60$ of a degree) of latitude.

The speed that a ship makes through the water for a given speed of rotation of her screws depends upon a number of factors: her condition of loading (the ship may be expected to move more slowly when heavily loaded than when empty), the resistance or push exerted on her superstructure and above-water hull by winds, the state of the sea (high waves may slow her down or may, at times, cause her screws to break the water surface, resulting in loss of propulsion efficiency), and the condition of her bottom (growth of sea plants or barnacles slows her down). Nevertheless, each ship has a *rated speed* at which she is expected to travel for a specific speed of rotation of her screws. This is the speed expected under normal conditions for each hull type, and is usually established by *speed trials* when the ship is new. The expression *maximum rated speed* refers to the highest speed at which the ship can conduct sustained operations.

Another term, *displacement,* is of interest. The weight of a ship is equal to the weight of the volume of water that she occupies when afloat. Thus, instead of speaking of the weight of a ship, the nautical term used refers to the weight of the volume of water that she displaces (or occupies). When speaking of the weight of a ship, seafarers will say, "She displaces 40,000 tons," or, "Her full load displacement is 40,000 tons."

All of these expressions are used by men and women of the Navy and Coast Guard when speaking of ships and their characteristics.

Bridge of an aircraft carrier. The interior of the superstructure is also used for conning the ship. This is the interior bridge with the crew at their stations.

The USS Oliver Hazard Perry *(FFG-7), USS* Antrim *(FFG-20), and USS* Jack Williams *(FFG-24)*

3.

MISSIONS AND ORGANIZATIONS

Both the Navy and Coast Guard are members of the United States armed services. They have similar uniforms, similar education and training programs, and they share the heritage and traditions of service to our nation and its people.

Despite their similarities, the Navy and Coast Guard have different missions and tasks to perform for the country. As a result, they do not have the same types of ships. Let's examine some of their similarities and differences.

The U.S. Navy is a member of the Defense Department. The Navy's primary mission is the defense of the United States and its allies. Protecting our nation from attack, preserving the freedom of the seas, projecting appropriate military power when required to discourage aggression and preserve the peace, these are the essential reasons for maintaining a strong Navy. Most Navy ships are warships. They are designed to meet and defeat any enemy, to "go in harm's way" when required in carrying out a mission.

The U.S. Coast Guard, on the other hand, is normally in the Department of Transportation. In time of war, or when the President so orders, the Coast Guard reports to the U.S. Navy and assists in fighting the enemies of the United States. In recent years, the Coast Guard commanders of the Atlantic and Pacific areas were designated commanders of the Maritime Defense Zones, Atlantic and Pacific. For this assignment they report to the Navy Fleet commanders, Atlantic and Pacific. Their responsibilities include: (1) wartime operations in and around U.S. harbors and coasts; (2) defense plans for the Maritime Defense Zones; (3) protection of U.S. coasts and harbors. The primary peacetime missions of the Coast Guard are: enforcement of maritime law, promotion and assurance of maritime safety, and defense readiness. The types and characteristics of Coast Guard vessels reflect the variety of tasks assigned. Even though they are not primarily warships, most are well armed and able to fight alongside Navy units when so ordered in time of war. Coast Guard vessels exemplify speed and the ability to respond to all requirements under all conditions. Their motto is *Semper Paratus*—Always Ready.

Navy ships are organized into fleets, battle forces, battle groups, action groups, and task forces—all under the command of the Joint Chiefs of Staff, the Chief of Naval Operations, and the commanders responsible for worldwide operations of the U.S. armed forces. Submarines normally operate on their own, not as part of a group, but they are always responsive to control by higher level commanders. U.S. Navy ships are capable of many tasks and a wide variety of mission assignments. With their guns, missiles, and torpedoes—and their competent, well-trained crews—these ships are a strong deterrent to attack on the United States by any potential enemy.

The organization of the Coast Guard is more in keeping with its peacetime responsibilities. Headquartered in Washington, D.C., it has two area commands to direct operations—in the Atlantic, from New York, and in the Pacific, from San Francisco. Large cutters (those greater than 180 feet in length) report directly to the area commander. Smaller cutters and boats report to a district commander—there are ten Coast Guard districts covering the U.S. The Coast Guard is responsible for safety and law enforcement on all navigable waters of the United States—coastal ocean areas, navigable rivers, and navigable lakes.

Navy battle group under way

The USCGC Vigorous *(WMEC-627)*

The USS Fox *(CG-33) in the Pacific Ocean*

4. SHIP NAMES

Ships have names and numerical designations that contain a great deal of information. Just by seeing or hearing the name and number of a ship, a knowledgeable person can immediately identify the ship type and some of the characteristics.

Navy ships have four parts to their names. Consider the USS *Enterprise* (CVN-65). The first part, USS, stands for United States ship and is a part of the name of every commissioned ship in the U.S. Navy—that is, every ship that has been officially commissioned as a member of our Navy. Some Navy noncombatant support ships are operated by civilian crews (either civil service or contractor-provided) under control of the Military Sealift Command. These ships carry the designation USNS for United States naval ship, instead of the usual USS.

The second part, *Enterprise,* is the actual name. Names are assigned by rules that will be explained later. Since *Enterprise* is the name that was formerly carried by a number of famous ships in our history, those who are familiar with Navy history and tradition know that it now indicates the name of an aircraft carrier.

Island of **Enterprise**
showing hull number 65

The third part of the name, CVN, tells what type of ship this is. CV is the Navy designation for aircraft carriers, and N denotes a ship having nuclear propulsion.

Finally, the fourth part of the name, 65, is the hull number. Hull numbers are normally assigned in sequence for each type of ship; so 65 means that the *Enterprise* is the sixty-fifth major aircraft carrier commissioned in the history of the U.S. Navy. This number is also the number painted on the ship's bow (and the island and flight deck of an aircraft carrier), and so it is sometimes called the *bow number* as well.

Thus by the name USS *Enterprise* (CVN-65), we know that this is a commissioned ship of the U.S. Navy named *Enterprise* after one or more famous Navy ships of the past, that she is a nuclear-powered aircraft carrier and the sixty-fifth combatant aircraft carrier that has been commissioned in the Navy.

Each ship of the Navy may be identified in similar fashion, by anyone who knows the meanings of the ship names and designators.

Coast Guard vessels also have names that convey meanings about their types and characteristics. Let us consider the USCGC *Midgett* (WHEC-726).

The first part, USCGC, stands for United States Coast Guard cutter, and signifies that this is a commissioned vessel of the Coast Guard. The name *cutter* deserves some

explanation, since almost all Coast Guard vessels (those over 65 feet in overall length) are called cutters. The term originated in the British Revenue Service many years ago when they used small, fast sailing craft with *cutter rig* (fore-and-aft sail, mast stepped farther aft than in sloop rig) as *revenue cutters*. These were used in collecting His Majesty's revenues from ships that entered British waters. Early Coast Guard vessels in the U.S. Revenue Service were given the name *cutter* because of the similar function they had in the United States.

The *Midgett* is one of three *Hamilton*-class cutters named after Coast Guard heroes. Thus the second part of the designation—the actual name of the cutter—is the name of the person whose memory is being honored.

The third part, WHEC, indicates that the *Midgett* is a Coast Guard ship (W) and is a high-endurance cutter (HEC). The W designator on all Coast Guard ships is thought by many to be derived from "white-painted ships." Actually, it probably comes from an early routing indicator used in the days when the Coast Guard was a part of the Treasury Department. When mail was delivered to that department, letters were assigned (much like zip codes of today) to expedite their routing. W was the letter assigned for all Coast Guard mail, and that letter came to represent Coast Guard. Hence it was later used as a vessel designator.

USCGC **Midgett**
(WHEC-726)

The number 726 is the fourth part of the name and indicates that this is ship number 726 on the list of high-endurance cutters. Coast Guard vessels less than 100 feet long are usually classified according to the length of their hulls. In a unique numbering system, the first two digits of the hull number indicate the ship's length. For example, the USCGC *Point Hannon* (WPB-82355) is an 82-foot Point-class patrol boat.

These simple rules govern the assignment of ship and vessel names and designators for Navy and Coast Guard. All commissioned ships in both services carry names and designators. By remembering a few guidelines, anyone can recognize types of Navy and Coast Guard ships and vessels.

There is one important difference between the ships of the Navy and the Coast Guard—their color. Navy ships, since they must always be prepared for fighting, are camouflaged with gray colors that blend in with the mists and fogs encountered at sea. Coast Guard vessels, because of their rescue and law-enforcement missions, want to be clearly visible during normal peacetime operations, so most cutters have hulls and superstructures painted white. Their white color and two distinctive diagonal stripes (a broad international-orange stripe containing the Coast Guard emblem, and a narrow blue stripe) painted along the hull aft of the bow make them readily recognizable. This enhances their ability to carry out assigned missions of safety and law enforcement. Icebreakers with white hulls, however, would be difficult to see in the ice fields, so their hulls are painted red for high visibility, with white diagonal stripes. Buoy tenders' hulls are usually black with white superstructures.

Aerial view of a battleship firing broadside from her 16-inch guns

5.
HOW SHIPS ARE NAMED

Ships of the Navy are named by the Secretary of the Navy in accordance with traditional rules and customs. In 1819, Congress decided that "ships of the first class" would be named for the states of our country, and those of the second class (smaller) would be named for rivers. Still smaller ships would be named after U.S. cities. In 1858, the rules were relaxed and Congress allowed names to be assigned "by the Secretary of the Navy as the President shall direct." Until after World War II, it was customary to name submarines after fish, battleships after states, cruisers after cities, aircraft carriers after famous battles and famous earlier ships, and destroyers after dead Navy and Marine Corps heroes. Today the customs have changed somewhat, as indicated below.

AIRCRAFT CARRIERS

Aircraft carriers are named after famous ships formerly on the Navy list (USS *Enterprise*), or important battles (USS *Midway*). In recent years, carriers have also been named to honor presidents and distinguished leaders (USS *John F. Kennedy,* USS *Forrestal*).

BATTLESHIPS

Battleships are named for states (USS *New Jersey*). Since so few battleships remain in our Navy, this rule applies also to other capital ships (USS *Ohio,* a very large ballistic-missile [Trident] submarine; and USS *Virginia,* a nuclear-powered, guided-missile cruiser).

USS New Jersey *(BB-62) and USCGC* Munro *(WHEC-724) in company*

Guided missile destroyer USS Scott *(DDG-995)*

CRUISERS

Cruisers, formerly named for cities (only the USS *Long Beach* is still in commission from those days), are today frequently named after famous battles (USS *Valley Forge*). But in 1975, ships of large destroyer types were reclassified as cruisers and allowed to use their original names—those that had been assigned as destroyer names (USS *Leahy*). Guided-missile, nuclear-propelled cruisers are now being named for states (USS *Texas*).

DESTROYERS AND FRIGATES

Destroyers and frigates honor deceased heroes of the Navy, Marine Corps, and Coast Guard (USS *Spruance*, USS *Bronstein*). They may also be named for members of Congress and for secretaries and assistant secretaries of the Navy. The only destroyer type named for a living hero is the USS *Arleigh Burke* (DDG-51). Admiral Burke became famous in World War II; his nickname was "31-Knot Burke." He later served two terms as Chief of Naval Operations. He is universally respected and admired, hence the honor of naming after him a new ship and class. It is particularly appropriate that the Secretary of the Navy chose to name the most capable new destroyer after this outstanding destroyerman.

BALLISTIC-MISSILE SUBMARINES

Ballistic-missile submarines are named after distinguished Americans (USS *Thomas A. Edison,* USS *Sam Rayburn*). Because of the large missiles these boats carry, they are popularly known to Navy personnel as "boomers." The large Trident ballistic-missile submarines are named after states (USS *Ohio*).

SUBMARINES

Submarines, other than ballistic-missile boats, were formerly named after fish and other sea creatures (USS *Haddock,* USS *Seahorse*). Some honor distinguished Americans and members of Congress (USS *Sam Houston,* USS *Richard B. Russell*). The newest classes of attack submarines are named for cities of the United States (USS *Los Angeles* [SSN-688]).

In the U.S. Coast Guard, cutters' names are selected by the Commandant of the Coast Guard, based upon the recommendations of a naming board. When Coast Guard vessels are built to a new design, the naming board recommends the category (WMEC, for medium-endurance cutter, for example), and within that category, a number of names are suggested for all the vessels that will be in the class.

USCGC **Harriet Lane**
(WMEC-903)

A-7E Corsair II aircraft in formation over the USS Dwight D. Eisenhower (CVN-69)

6.
SHIP TYPES AND DESIGNATIONS

Navy ships of different types are given different letter designations. Although there is no exact meaning, the first letter usually is the initial of a word that describes the ship type. For example, auxiliary ships have designators beginning with the letter A. AD, the designation for destroyer tenders, could be interpreted as *auxiliary ship for destroyers*. Ships with L as the first letter in their designations are generally those used in amphibious warfare (landing ships). BB denotes battleships, DD destroyers, SS submarines, FF frigates, C cruisers, and CV aircraft carriers (carriers of heavier-than-air aircraft).

There are a few letters that are used for all types of ships: E before the designator means that the ship is experimental, G after a designator means that the ship is equipped with guided missiles, and N after the designator means the ship has nuclear propulsion. When the letter T precedes the designator, it means that the ship is a USNS (United States naval ship) and is operated by a civilian crew.

But the letters show only the ship type, not the class. Ship type means the basic category of ship, such as battleship (type BB), submarine (type SS), destroyer (type DD), and the like. However, within each type there may be a number of classes. Over a period of years, one or more ships of the same type may be built with essentially the same set of plans, meaning they will be in the same class. They are similar in length, beam, displacement, and general arrangement. Others of the same type may be built using a different design; these will be in a different class. Thus each destroyer is given an individual name, and also has a class to which she belongs. She may be one of any of several destroyer classes, such as the *Spruance* (DD-963) class or of the *Farragut* (DDG-37) class, meaning that she is similar to the other ships of that particular model, or class. For example, the USS *Fletcher* (DD-992) is a *Spruance*-class destroyer.

Classes are usually named after the first ship of the new design, and the hull numbers are usually in sequence following the first ship. How many ships are in each class depends upon the shipbuilding program that remains in effect until a new design or model is approved and a new class started.

The Coast Guard uses the term *vessels* to describe all of its waterborne craft, calling those over 65 feet in length *cutters* and those under 65 feet *boats* or *craft*. Coast Guard vessels also have class names that follow a certain pattern, and letter and number designators. Their letter designators, like those of the Navy, have no exact mean-

USCGC **Mellon**
(WHEC-717)

ing, but they are similar to the words that describe the vessel type.

All Coast Guard designators begin with the letter W; this, as explained earlier, dates from the use of that letter to route mail to the Coast Guard when it was still in the Department of the Treasury. The letters that follow describe the vessel type. AGB means an icebreaker. HEC and MEC mean a high-endurance cutter and a medium-endurance cutter, respectively. IX means a training cutter. Buoy tenders are an important type of Coast Guard vessel; their designators are LB for large buoy tenders, LI for inland tenders, LM for coastal buoy tenders, and LR for river buoy tenders.

The Coast Guard also uses a large fleet of boats to patrol inland and coastal waters. These are frequently welcome sights to yachts and fishing vessels in distress—they offer assistance and a tow to the nearest harbor. The designator for patrol boats is WPB.

Each of these letter designations is followed by a hull number, just as in the Navy. This number identifies the sequence in which the cutter or boat fits into each Coast Guard type and class. WPBs of less than 100-foot length, as explained earlier, have hull numbers that include the length.

There are many ship and vessel types in the U.S. Navy and Coast Guard, each with a letter designation. Each type may contain a number of different classes, but the class cannot always be determined from the letter designations alone. Listed on the following pages are the most common, or representative, types of Navy ships and Coast Guard vessels, with their letter designators.

Designation	Navy ship type	Designation	Navy ship type
AD	Destroyer tender	CVN	Aircraft carrier (nuclear-powered)
AE	Ammunition ship	DD	Destroyer
AFS	Combat stores ship	DDG	Guided missile destroyer
AO	Oiler	FF	Frigate
AOE	Fast combat support ship	FFG	Guided missile frigate
AOR	Replenishment oiler	LCC	Amphibious command ship
AR	Repair ship	LHA	Amphibious assault ship
ARS	Salvage ship	LKA	Amphibious cargo ship
AS	Submarine tender	LPD	Amphibious transport, dock
ASR	Submarine rescue ship	LST	Landing ship, tank
ATF	Fleet ocean tug	MSO	Minesweeper, ocean
ATS	Salvage tug	PHM	Patrol hydrofoil (missile)
BB	Battleship	SS	Submarine
CG	Guided missile cruiser	SSBN	Ballistic missile submarine (nuclear-powered)
CGN	Guided missile cruiser (nuclear-powered)		
CV	Aircraft carrier	SSN	Attack submarine (nuclear-powered)

Designation	Coast Guard vessel type
WAGB	Polar class icebreaker
WHEC	High-endurance cutter
WIX	Training cutter
WLB	Buoy tender
WLI	Buoy tender, inland
WLIC	Construction tender, inland
WLM	Buoy tender, coastal
WLR	Buoy tender, river
WMEC	Medium-endurance cutter
WPB	Patrol boat
WTGB	Icebreaking tug

USCGC **Eagle** *(WIX-327)—sail drill for midshipmen*

The USS New Jersey *(BB-62) under way alongside the USS* Dwight D. Eisenhower *(CVN-69)*

Catapult launch of F-14 aboard USS **Ranger** *(CV-61)*

7.
AIRCRAFT CARRIERS

The aircraft carrier is the most important member of the modern Navy team and the center of today's powerful battle groups. It was the first new type of warship produced in this century; its introduction revolutionized naval warfare. Today the aircraft carrier is the principal surface ship that assures the U.S. Navy's control of the seas in support of our national objectives.

A carrier is a mobile air base that can operate in international waters on all parts of the globe; with great speed, it can be on the scene and in action. The carrier's mission is to use her aircraft to control the air around and above the operating area. With squadrons of fighter, bomber, and reconnaissance aircraft aboard, the carrier provides close air support for troops ashore, protection of friendly ships and boats, and reconnaissance information on enemy movements and installations. The reconnaissance aircraft also provide detection and constant surveillance of all submarines and surface ships over a large area, calling on fighter and attack aircraft when necessary. A carrier battle group can apply the precise force required in any situation.

The most modern carriers are the nuclear-powered type—that is, those having nuclear reactors as the heart of their main-propulsion machinery. Using a controlled nuclear-fission reaction (instead of an oil-fired boiler) to generate heat, which produces steam to drive the turbines, they have a long-lasting, readily available source of power. These ships can carry more aviation fuel and aviation ordnance than those that rely on oil, because a nuclear-powered carrier does not need any space in its hull for a supply of propulsion fuel oil. The Navy has five nuclear carriers in service today, with two more being built and two planned for future service.

With their speedy response and their high degree of logistics independence, these nuclear-powered carriers form the heart of the Navy's quick-reaction forces for the next three decades. They can move rapidly to areas of potential crisis without delaying for logistic-support forces that carry fuel oil. These carriers represent a national capability to bring to bear effective military strength in distant areas with closely controlled, versatile forces.

USS *Nimitz* (CVN-68)

The *Nimitz* is the lead ship of our most modern nuclear-powered aircraft carriers. These are the largest, most powerful warships in the world. They are 1,090 feet long, have a beam of 252 feet at the widest point of the flight deck, and a maximum draft of 38 feet. They can accom-

USS **Nimitz** *(CVN-68)*
with A-7 aircraft

modate 6,300 officers and enlisted personnel, including the air wing personnel. Their combat-load displacement is 95,000 tons. *Nimitz*-class carriers have two reactors and nuclear fuel for as long as thirteen years of normal operations—the equivalent of 11 million barrels of propulsion fuel oil. With a rated speed in excess of 30 knots, each of these ships can support a modern air wing of about 85 planes. The *Nimitz* was delivered in 1975, and commenced her first deployment in July 1976. The other ships of the class now in active service are the *Dwight D. Eisenhower* (CVN-69), *Carl Vinson* (CVN-70), and *Theodore Roosevelt* (CVN-71). Two additional ships of this class are being built: the *Abraham Lincoln* (CVN-72) and *George Washington* (CVN-73). They are expected to join the fleet in the early 1990s. Two more CVNs, to be named the *John C. Stennis* (CVN-74) and *United States* (CVN-75), have been authorized and are expected to join the fleet in the late 1990s.

USS *Enterprise* (CVN-65)

The *Enterprise* is the first nuclear-powered aircraft carrier ever built. She was commissioned in November 1961, and has since made a number of remarkable records. In 1964, the *Enterprise,* with Nuclear Task Force One, circumnavigated the world, cruising over 30,000 miles without taking on fuel or provisions. Theoretically, she could cruise eight times around the globe without the need to renew her nuclear fuel. She is 1,100 feet in length, with a maximum beam (flight deck) of 257 feet and a maximum draft of 39 feet. Her flight deck has an area of about 4½ acres; this means that three football fields could fit on it. The main engines have eight pressurized-water nuclear reactors feeding steam to four steam turbines that generate up to 360,000 horsepower, which can drive the ship at speeds greater than 30 knots. She can accommodate a crew and air wing of more than 6,000, and normally carries about 85 aircraft. Full-load displacement is approximately 90,000 tons.

USS Enterprise *(CVN-65)*

USS *Kitty Hawk* (CV-63)

Commissioned in April 1961, this is the first of three modern large carriers—not nuclear-powered—in the *Kitty Hawk* class. Others in this class are the *Constellation* (CV-64) and *America* (CV-66). An improved version, the *John F. Kennedy* (CV-67), was commissioned in 1968. She has approximately the same dimensions as the *Kitty Hawk* class, but because her full-load displacement was increased to 87,000 tons, she is the only ship in a separate class. The *Kitty Hawk* is 1,048 feet long, with a maximum beam of 252 feet and a 37-foot maximum draft. Main engines capable of generating 280,000 horsepower give her a rated speed of over 30 knots. She carries a crew plus air wing of over 4,000 and has more than 80 aircraft. Her full-load displacement is 80,000 tons.

USS **Kitty Hawk** *(CV-63)*

USS **Ranger** *(CV-61)*

USS *Ranger* (CV-61)

The *Ranger* is one of four ships of the *Forrestal* class, first ships constructed from the keel up as carriers after World War II. With a length of 1,046 feet, beam (flight deck) of 270 feet, and draft of 37 feet, she displaces about 78,000 tons, full load. She has a crew of some 3,000 officers and enlisted personnel, and can also accommodate an air wing of 3,400 officers and enlisted personnel. With 280,000 shaft horsepower from her four steam-turbine main power plant (eight boilers), she has a rated speed of 34 knots. Other ships in this class are: the *Forrestal* (CV-59), *Saratoga* (CV-60), and *Independence* (CV-62).

U.S. Navy ships in formation: USS **Deyo** *(DD-989),* USS **Iowa** *(BB-61),* USS **Comte de Grasse** *(DD-974), and* USS **Yorktown** *(CG-48).*

8.
BATTLESHIPS AND CRUISERS

Battleships and cruisers are designed to be able to fight battles at sea against enemy ships and aircraft, using their guns, missiles, and armor plate to best advantage. Cruisers are used primarily to screen carrier battle groups, protecting them from air and submarine attack. Battleships and aircraft carriers have limited antiaircraft warfare (AAW) and antisubmarine warfare (ASW) equipment, so they require AAW/ASW escort, usually cruisers, destroyers, and frigates. Both battleships and cruisers are equipped with surface-to-surface missiles (SSM), and thus are able to fire considerably beyond the range of their guns. Their mission is that of a surface-action group: to engage enemy ships with gun and missile fire, to deliver heavy and continuous bombardment against enemy shore installations, and to provide protection to battle groups against enemy ships. In addition, they frequently serve as flagships and carry both the staff and the communications equipment necessary for the battle group commander to conduct at-sea operations. With their high sustained speed, even in adverse weather and heavy seas, the battleships can respond rapidly to threatened areas where they may be needed.

The former designations of heavy cruiser (CA) and light cruiser (CL), which referred to the size of the main battery guns installed, are no longer in use: all cruisers today have missile batteries, not guns, as their main armament. The cruisers in today's Navy include those classes formerly known as destroyer leaders or guided missile frigates (DL, DLG, and DLGN), which were similar in size to earlier cruisers and so have been redesignated as CG and CGN.

In recent years, the Navy's four remaining World War II battleships have been recalled to active duty. They offer heavy gunfire support of forces ashore, and their size makes them appropriate to serve as flagships and command centers. In addition to their powerful 16-inch guns, these large, heavily armored ships are ideal for directing combat operations and for providing the necessary storage space and stable platform for launching a variety of missiles. These four are the only battleships in the world in active service.

USS *Wisconsin* (BB-64)

This is one of four *Iowa*-class battleships that were decommissioned and placed "in mothballs" after World War II. The other three are the *Iowa* (BB-61), *New Jersey* (BB-62), and *Missouri* (BB-63). All four have now been recommissioned and are in active service, with

USS **Wisconsin** *(BB-64)*

two in the Atlantic Fleet and two in the Pacific Fleet. They are 887 feet in length, with beam of 108 feet and draft of 38 feet maximum. Their full-load displacement is about 58,000 tons, and the current (peacetime) crew consists of 1,550 officers and enlisted personnel. With main engines rated at 212,000 shaft horsepower, these ships have a rated speed of 33 knots. Their nine 16-inch guns can each hurl a 2,700-pound projectile more than 20 miles with pinpoint precision, giving strong gunfire sup-

port to U.S. operating forces. Each has also been fitted out with thirty-two Tomahawk surface-to-surface missiles and sixteen Harpoon cruise missiles. One outstanding characteristic of these magnificent ships is their protective armor—17 inches thick on turrets and conning tower, 12 inches thick along the sides, and 6 inches thick on armor decks. Vital spaces are protected against bombs, missiles, and projectiles by these massive installations of steel armor.

USS *Texas* (**CGN-39**)

The second ship of the *Virginia* class of eight planned nuclear-powered guided-missile cruisers, the *Texas* is 585 feet in length, with a beam of 63 feet and draft of 29 feet. She displaces 11,000 tons (full load) and is manned by 38 officers and 459 enlisted personnel. Ships of this class are powered by two nuclear reactors that give them a speed of over 30 knots. Their armament consists of Tartar/ Standard surface-to-air missiles (SAM), eight Harpoon surface-to-surface missiles (SSM), eight Tomahawk cruise missiles, antisubmarine rockets (ASROC), two 5-inch/54-caliber guns, and four torpedo tubes. Other active ships in this class are the *Virginia* (CGN-38), *Mississippi* (CGN-40), and *Arkansas* (CGN-41).

USS Texas *(CGN-39)*

USS *Ticonderoga* (CG-47)

This is the lead ship of a new class of Aegis cruisers—so called because they carry the Aegis weapon system, a very complex, computer-controlled radar and missile system designed to provide the finest antiaircraft protection. Ships of this class are named for battles, except for CG-51, which was named to honor Thomas S. Gates, deceased former Secretary of the Navy. The *Ticonderoga*-class design is a modification of *Spruance*-class ships, and plans are for a total of twenty-seven of these very capable, non-nuclear cruisers. The *Ticonderoga* was commissioned in 1983. She has a crew of 364 officers and enlisted personnel. The ships of this class have a full-load displacement of 9,500 tons. In all other respects, their characteristics are similar to those of the *Spruance* (DD-963) class. *Ticonderoga*-class ships provide carrier battle groups with strong defense against aircraft and cruise-missile attacks. They are the most capable antiair warfare (AAW) ships in the world.

USS Ticonderoga *(CG-47)*

USS **Jouett** *(CG-29)*

USS *Jouett* (CG-29)

This is one of the *Belknap* class of nine cruisers, former DLGs reclassified as CGs in June 1975. They are designed as screening ships for carrier battle groups. Equipped with Terrier/Standard AAW missiles and with antisubmarine rocket launchers, they are excellent for operations against both enemy aircraft and submarines.

They also carry eight Harpoon missiles for surface-to-surface engagements. Displacement is 7,900 tons, length is 547 feet, beam is 55 feet, and the four-boiler, two steam-turbine, main power plant generates 85,000 shaft horsepower; it is capable of producing speeds rated at 33 knots.

USS **Arleigh Burke** *(DDG-51)*

9. DESTROYERS AND FRIGATES

Ships of the destroyer type are the most versatile of our Navy's warships. Their duties include bombarding enemy shore installations, blockading shipping, escorting Navy battle groups and merchant-ship convoys, and providing vital defense against enemy submarines and aircraft. Lightly constructed, fast and highly maneuverable, these "tin cans" (so called because of their thin steel, unarmored hulls) depend upon speed and firepower rather than armor for protection.

Frigates are a recent addition to the fleet. In post–World War II days, the destroyer-leader type (DL) became the frigate type. In 1975, when the large DLs were reclassified as cruisers and the small ones as destroyers, the name *frigate* was given to the existing destroyer-escort (DE) type. DEs no longer exist as a type in today's Navy.

The missions of the frigates and destroyers are many. They provide gunfire and missile support to forces afloat and ashore, and their speed and maneuverability make them excellent patrol and intercept ships to prevent enemy ships from entering protected zones. The name *destroyer* evolved from their first role, that of torpedo-boat destroyer. They are also excellent defensive ships. With their missiles and dual-purpose guns, they can defend against both surface targets and air targets. A most important mission is that of providing protection against enemy submarines. All DDs and FFs are equipped with sonar (sound navigation and ranging) equipment for detecting and tracking submerged submarines. They also carry a number of weapons especially designed for attacking enemy submarines. With their excellent speed and maneuverability, these ships are able to react quickly to the submarine's evasive tactics, bringing their weapons within range to destroy the enemy. Finally, their mission includes the use of torpedoes against enemy ships if such attacks become necessary.

The Navy needs large numbers of these versatile ships, both in peacetime and wartime. The U.S. Navy today has well over 100 DDs and FFs in commission. New classes of both types are equipped with the latest missiles, electronics equipment, and other advanced-technology devices for maximum performance of their many and varied missions.

USS *Arleigh Burke* (DDG-51)

Now under construction, this is the first ship of a fine new class named after Admiral Arleigh Burke, the famed destroyerman of World War II who was known as

31-Knot Burke for his tendency to proceed into battle at full speed. The *Burke* class will consist of some twenty-nine ships, with three now being built, five more authorized, and twenty-one planned for future programs. These ships will have a length of 466 feet, a beam of 59 feet, and a full-load draft of 31 feet. Their armament will consist of eight Harpoon antiship missiles, ninety cells for vertical launch of a combination of Standard AAW, Tomahawk SSM, and ASROC ASW missiles. They will also carry a single 5-inch, 54-caliber gun forward and two 20-millimeter Phalanx rapid fire CIWS (close in weapon system) machine guns. Main engines powered by four gas turbines will generate 100,000 shaft horsepower, capable of driving the ships at speeds of over 30 knots. With 23 officers and a crew of 302, these ships will be among the most capable surface combatants in the world for the next two decades. Their role will be to use their fine AAW capability and missiles to support the Aegis cruisers in defense of carrier battle groups against aircraft and missile attack.

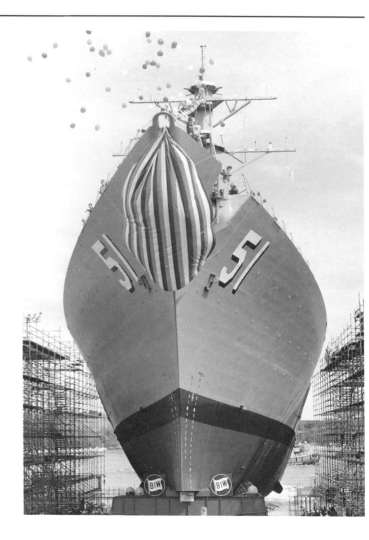

USS Arleigh Burke *(DDG-51)*

USS *Callaghan* (DDG-994)

The four ships of the *Kidd* class, including the *Callaghan,* were ordered by the Iranian government in 1974, before the overthrow of the shah of Iran. Instead of delivering the completed ships to Iran after the shah was deposed, they were accepted as members of the U.S. Navy. These ships are variations of the *Spruance*-class design, but they are optimized for general warfare (antisurface warfare, antiair warfare, and antisubmarine warfare) instead of just the antisubmarine warfare specialty of the *Spruance* class. As a result, their displacement is a heavier 9,500 tons; however, their other dimensions are the same as those of the *Spruance* class. Their armament, consisting of two twin Standard SAM launchers, eight Harpoon SSMs, two 5-inch guns, and two 20-millimeter Phalanx machine guns, is greater than that of the *Spruance* class, but their speeds, crews, and other characteristics are about the same. These ships were commissioned in the U.S. Navy in 1981 and 1982. They are the most capable destroyers in the fleet at this time.

USS Callaghan *(DDG-994)*

USS Richard E. Byrd *(DDG-23)*

USS *Richard E. Byrd* (DDG-23)

A member of the *Charles F. Adams* class of twenty-three general-purpose AAW and ASW destroyers, the *Byrd* was commissioned in 1964. Although the basic hull design is the same for all of the *Adams* class (DDG-2 through 24), there are some differences in the armament and detection equipments on board the different ships of the class. Their major characteristics are: length, 432 feet; beam, 47 feet; maximum draft, 22 feet; full-load displacement, 4,500 tons. Their 90,000 horsepower boiler, steam-turbine engines drive them at a rated speed of 31 knots. Each crew numbers 354 officers and enlisted personnel. Basic armament for the class is two single-mount 5-inch guns, one forward and one aft, an ASROC installation amidships, and a twin Tartar/Standard missile launcher aft. They are also equipped to launch Harpoon surface-to-surface missiles.

USS *Farragut* (DDG-37)

Originally designated a frigate (DLG-6), the *Farragut* is lead ship of ten DDGs of a class commissioned between 1959 and 1961. The *Farragut* class, DDG-37 through 46, consists of *single enders* (guided missiles either forward or aft, not both) with a 5-inch gun forward and twin Terrier/Standard (SAM) launchers aft. Ships of the *Farragut* class also are equipped with eight Harpoon missiles for use against surface targets. Full-load displacement is about 6,000 tons. Length is 512 feet, beam 52 feet, and maximum draft 25 feet. With four boilers providing steam to two turbines and generating 85,000 horsepower, the rated speed is 33 knots.

USS *Fletcher* (DD-992)

The *Fletcher* is one of thirty-one active members of the *Spruance* class of ASW destroyers. Although they were designed primarily for ASW, SAM and SSM capabilities have been added to the ships, providing significant AAW and anti-surface warfare (ASuW) potential. They are 560 feet long, with a beam of 55 feet and draft of 29 feet. Their armament includes Sea Sparrow, Harpoon, and Tomahawk missiles; two 5-inch guns; and ASROCs. The crew consists of about 330 officers and enlisted personnel. The first major U.S. Navy ships to be powered by gas turbines (the four gas turbines generate 80,000 horsepower), these ships have a rated speed of 32.5 knots.

USS Farragut *(DDG-37)*

USS **Fletcher** *(DD-992)*

Spruance-class ships have reversible-pitch propellers, giving them a high degree of maneuverability.

USS *Copeland* (FFG-25)

This ship is one of the *Oliver Hazard Perry* (FFG-7) class of guided-missile frigates—a new design capable of operating effectively against air, surface, and subsurface threats. Fifty ships of this class have been built; thirty-five are now in active service with the fleet, and fifteen are assigned to the Mobilization Forces. The ships of this class displace 3,600 tons, full load, and are 445 feet long, with a beam of 45 feet and a draft of 24 feet. Powered by two gas turbines that can develop 40,000 shaft horsepower, they have a sustained-speed rating of over 28 knots. They are equipped with Harpoon and Standard missiles, and are capable of firing Tomahawk missiles as well. In addition, they have both hull-mounted sonar and a towed-array system for detection of submarines, along with two triple-tube torpedo mounts, and two LAMPS helicopters for attacking enemy submarines after they have been detected and localized.

USS **Copeland** *(FFG-25)*

USS Knox *(FF-1052)*

USS *Knox* (FF-1052)

The largest of the frigate classes, the *Knox* is lead ship of a class of forty-six ships, of which thirty-nine are now in the fleet. Displacing 4,200 tons, full load, with a length of 438 feet, beam of 47 feet, and full-load draft of 25 feet, these ships are the equivalent of modern destroyers in all respects except speed and firepower. Their two boilers and steam turbines generate about 35,000 shaft horsepower, giving them a rated speed of 27 knots. The ships of this class have a massive sonar that projects beneath the bow.

USS Georgia (SSBN-729)

10. SUBMARINES

Submarines have long played an important part in warfare at sea. From their earliest uses for patrol and scouting, planting mines and other explosive charges, and attacking enemy shipping, they have relied primarily upon their ability to stay hidden beneath the surface—and that is still one of their most important assets. Known as the Silent Service, they can suppress both acoustic and electromagnetic emissions; they use the ocean as a blanket to hide them from friends and enemies alike—for frequently at sea it is difficult to distinguish one from the other.

The addition of nuclear power has greatly increased the importance of submarines. Now they are true submersibles that can stay under the ocean for weeks or months and can cruise at great speeds while submerged. This was not possible when submarines relied on diesel engines, which required air and fuel, and electric storage batteries that needed frequent recharging. Since they now can be designed for almost unlimited submerged operations, nuclear-powered submarines can have hull forms especially tailored to high submerged speeds. For this reason, modern submarines are faster when submerged than when running on the surface.

The use of atomic fuel gives a submarine great cruising range at top speed without the need for frequent refueling. Some strategists believe that future navies may be largely submarine-type ships, retaining their original missions but relying on staying submerged in order to be protected from enemy missiles.

Today's Navy attack submarines (SSNs) have a number of missions. They perform tactical functions of patrol, reconnaissance, enemy shipping attack, and enemy submarine detection and attack. They are also sometimes used as radar picket stations in locations near enemy coastlines, and as rescue stations for downed aircraft crews just off of enemy coasts.

The formidable fleet of ballistic-missile submarines (SSBNs) perform the vital role of *strategic deterrence*. With about forty active SSBNs armed with long-range ballistic missiles, the U.S. Navy keeps at least one-third of its boomers deployed in the oceans of the world. They can remain submerged and hidden from detection in ocean waters well within range of any potential enemy's important targets. The fact that the U.S. Navy has this capability is a strong deterrent to any enemy's attempt to start a surprise war, hoping to knock out all U.S. offensive weapons in the first attack. Thus the well-hidden SSBNs, armed with powerful missiles containing nuclear warheads, are an important U.S. weapon for the prevention of future wars.

USS Tennessee *(SSBN-734)*

USS *Tennessee* (SSBN-734)

This is one of ten *Ohio*-class fleet ballistic-missile (FBM) submarines in active service. Ten additional boats of this class are now either under construction or in the planning stages. They are named after U.S. states except for the SSBN-730, which was named to honor the late Senator Henry M. Jackson. These are the largest submarines ever built by the U.S. Navy. The *Tennessee* has a length of 560 feet and a beam of 42 feet. Her draft is 36 feet (surfaced), and her displacement is 18,750 tons (submerged). Powered by a single pressurized-water nuclear reactor that provides the steam for two steam turbines driving her single propeller shaft, she is designed for 60,000 shaft horsepower and a submerged speed of about 30 knots. She carries a crew of 15 officers and 141 enlisted personnel. The *Ohio*-class boats are equipped with twenty-four missile tubes for the Trident intercontinental ballistic missiles, which have ranges of over 5,000 miles. In addition, this class carries a number of Mark 48 torpedoes and has four torpedo tubes to fire them. In addition to launching Tridents with destructive warheads, the missile tubes can be used to launch defensive interceptor missiles, possibly as part of the Star Wars strategic defense initiative (SDI) defensive system. They may also have a role in launching other types of satellites for emergency communications, reconnaissance, and similar operations.

USS *James Monroe* (SSBN-622)

A member of the *Lafayette* class, the *James Monroe* was commissioned in 1963. Originally this class was planned to include thirty-one ships, all named after distinguished men of history. Subsequent variations of the basic design have created three distinct classes: the *Lafayette* (SSBN-616) class, *James Madison* (SSBN-627) class, and *Benjamin Franklin* (SSBN-640) class. About twenty-nine are now in active service with the fleet. All displace 8,250 tons submerged and are 425 feet long with a beam of 33 feet and draft of 31 feet. Each has a single reactor and twin steam turbines driving a single propeller shaft with power output rated at 15,000 shaft horsepower. Their speed is approximately 20 knots on the surface and 25 knots when submerged. All boomers of these classes carry sixteen ballistic-missile launching tubes, some capable of handling the Poseidon and others the Trident missiles. In addition, all have four torpedo tubes for Mark 48 torpedoes. These submarines are operated by crews of 143 officers and enlisted personnel. Their nuclear-reactor cores provide each boat with energy for approximately 400,000 miles of travel.

USS James Monroe
(SSBN-622)

USS *Seawolf* (SSN-21)

The SSNs are called *attack submarines* because that is their prime mission—to attack enemy ships and enemy submarines. A total of 100 SSNs is planned for the U.S. Navy. This is the newest attack submarine, designed with improved quieting and higher submerged speed than existing SSNs. The new class is designated SSN-21 to indicate that it is planned as the attack submarine of the twenty-first century. The *Seawolf* is the first of this class of twenty-five boats planned for operations beginning in the late 1990s. Her designed displacement is about 9,000 tons, with a length of 326 feet, beam of 40 feet, and draft on the surface of 36 feet. With a single reactor and two steam turbines, this submarine will develop 60,000 shaft horsepower, capable of driving the boat at 35 knots while submerged. She will carry Mark 48 torpedoes, Harpoon and Tomahawk missiles, all fired from her eight torpedo tubes located amidships. Her crew is planned to be 130 officers and enlisted personnel. The *Seawolf* class will be the replacement for existing *Los Angeles*–class SSNs as they reach the end of their thirty-year useful life.

USS *Oklahoma City* (SSN-723)

The *Oklahoma City* is a member of the *Los Angeles* (SSN-688) class—the Navy's largest class of nuclear submarines, with sixty-six boats built or planned. All are named after U.S. cities except the *Hyman G. Rickover* (SSN-709), named after Admiral Rickover, who contributed significantly to the development of the nuclear Navy. The *Oklahoma City* displaces about 6,900 tons (sub-

USS **Seawolf** *(SSN-21)*

USS **Oklahoma City** *(SSN-723)*

USS **Sturgeon** *(SSN-637)*

merged), has a length of 360 feet, beam of 33 feet, and draft of 32 feet. Her reactor and twin steam turbines generate 30,000 shaft horsepower to drive her at speeds exceeding 30 knots submerged. In addition to her four torpedo tubes for attacking enemy ships and submarines, she carries Harpoon and Tomahawk surface-to-surface missiles (SSMs) launched from twelve vertical-launch tubes. Other boats of this class can also launch the SSMs from their torpedo tubes if they have not yet been fitted with vertical-launch tubes.

USS *Sturgeon* (SSN-637)

After the *Los Angeles* class, this is the largest class of SSNs in the Navy. They are very capable boats, even though somewhat older. They are smaller than later classes, and all have been fitted with a complete under-ice operational capability that includes strengthening features necessary for breaking through thick ice. The *Sturgeon* has a length of 292 feet, beam of 32 feet, and draft of 29 feet. Her submerged displacement is about 4,800 tons. A main power plant of 15,000 shaft horsepower gives her a speed of about 30 knots, submerged. She is equipped with Mark 48 torpedoes and Harpoon and Tomahawk SSMs, all launched from four amidships torpedo tubes.

USS **Wasp** *(LHD-1) with Harrier aircraft*

11.
AMPHIBIOUS WARFARE SHIPS

The U.S. Navy developed the techniques of modern amphibious warfare in World War II, and has been improving upon them since then. To take and hold territory requires that troops be put on enemy-held shores, equipped to overcome enemy troops and to sustain operations for an indefinite period. The role of the Navy's amphibious warfare ships is to transport troops and their equipment from their bases to enemy shores, and to land them safely and efficiently. To do so requires a number of different types of ships, each with its own part to play as a member of the Navy's amphibious warfare team.

New ships with improved carrying capacity and speed have been developed for modern amphibious warfare. The advent of the helicopter, and its increasing use aboard ships, has played an important part in landing troops. Helicopters allow rapid transport of the first wave of Marines to the battle area. Landing behind enemy lines, they can quickly establish a beachhead for oncoming waves of assault boats carrying heavy support equipment (tanks, trucks, artillery) and other troops.

The primary mission of the amphibious force is to land troops on enemy-controlled territory. Using command

USS Essex (LHD-2)

ships (LCC) to direct and control landings; assault ships (LHA, LHD, and LPH) to provide helicopter support; transports (LPD) to carry personnel; landing craft carriers (LKA) to carry troops, supplies, and equipment; tank landing ships (LST) to transport the heavy tanks and trucks to the beach; and a variety of support ships, the Navy has become adept at carrying out this mision. The amphibious ships are well supported by gunfire and missiles from escorting cruisers and destroyers, and by bombing and strafing of enemy positions ashore by aircraft from nearby carriers. Units of battle groups provide air defense and defense against submarines.

USS *Essex* (LHD-2)

The *Essex* is the second ship of a new class (*Wasp* class) of large amphibious assault ships designed to carry helicopters and Harrier vertical/short takeoff and landing (VSTOL) aircraft. The first two of the class, the *Wasp* and *Essex,* were named after famous warships of the past. Six LHDs are now either being built or planned. They have a displacement of approximately 40,000 tons, full load, with overall length of 844 feet, beam of 140 feet, and draft of 27 feet. These ships are equipped with a docking well in the stern to carry different types of landing craft and discharge them, fully loaded, when the landing area is reached. Boiler and steam turbines driving two shafts with some 70,000 horsepower give *Wasp*-class ships a rated speed of over 22 knots. The *Essex* has a crew of about 1,080 officers and enlisted personnel. She can carry over 1850 troops, 40 AV-8 Harrier VSTOL aircraft, and a number of helicopters. In addition, the *Wasp*-class ships will have extensive medical facilities, with six operating rooms and 600 hospital beds in each. They are similar to the *Tarawa*-class LHAs, and will eventually replace them in the fleet as the LHAs reach the end of their useful life.

USS *Denver* (LPD-9)

The *Denver* is a member of the *Austin* (LPD-4) class. There are eleven ships in this class of *amphibious transport, dock;* they are named after U.S. cities. These are 17,000-ton full-load displacement ships, 569 feet in length, with an 84-foot beam and a 23-foot draft. Steam turbine–driven twin shafts generate 24,000 shaft horsepower, which is capable of driving the ships at rated speeds of 20 knots—allowing for fast approaches to the assault area. They are essentially troop carriers, with a capacity for transporting 900 Marines and their equipment to landing areas, then unloading them by means of helicopters and landing craft. These ships, like the LSD types, can launch preloaded landing craft from the well deck in the stern. The platform above the well deck is the landing pad for helicopters that may be used to take combat forces ashore. *Austin*-class ships normally carry four large helicopters to ferry personnel and cargo ashore.

USS **Denver** *(LPD-9)*

USS Inchon *(LPH-12)*

USS *Inchon* (LPH-12)

This is one of the *Iwo Jima* (LPH-2) class of seven ships named for famous battles. Built to operate helicopters, the *Inchon* can carry about twenty-five helicopters of various types. The designation LPH is sometimes thought to stand for *landing platform for helicopters,* but this is incorrect. L indicates an amphibious ship, P designates a transport (personnel carrier), and H shows that it is a helicopter carrier. These ships are 602 feet in length, have a beam of 104 feet (at the flight deck), and a draft of 26 feet. They displace 18,000 tons, fully loaded, and are capable of speeds of 22 knots. They can accommodate some 2,000 troops and their equipment, with the ability to ferry them ashore by helicopter lift. In addition to this troop-carrying ability, these ships have extensive medical facilities and a sick bay that includes 300 beds.

USS *Charleston* (LKA-113)

The LKA types are known as landing craft carriers because of the twenty-four landing craft used to ferry cargo to the assault area when needed. The most vital cargo (food, guns, ammunition, clothing, medical supplies) is stowed near the top of the holds so it can be sent to the beachhead with the first assault waves, followed by supplies necessary to sustain an operation after the beachhead is secured. The many booms on the main deck are for off-loading the boats and then lifting the heavy cargo from deep in the holds of the ship into the boats. The *Charleston* is the first in her class of five ships. Displacing almost 19,000 tons when fully loaded, she has a length of 576 feet, a beam of 62 feet, and a maximum draft of 26 feet. With a single shaft and 22,000-horsepower steam turbine, she can travel at speeds of greater than 20 knots. This is the first class of ships designed especially as LKAs; other cargo carriers have been converted merchant ships.

USS Charleston *(LKA-113)*

USS *Whidbey Island* (LSD-41)

The *Whidbey Island* class of eight ships (three in active service, five being built) will be supplemented with six more of the same general dimensions, but modified to have a smaller docking well and larger troop and cargo space. This class is built around a dry-dock-like well that may be flooded or drained as desired. Thus the ship may be used as a dry dock for small ships and boats, or, as more often happens, she may receive fully loaded landing craft in the flooded well deck, which is then pumped dry for transport to the assault area. When in the landing area, the crew floods the dock and opens the stern gate, allowing the craft to become waterborne and depart rapidly for the beach. The *Whidbey Island* has a full-load displacement of approximately 16,000 tons. Her length is 610 feet, beam is 84 feet, and draft is 20 feet. She has four diesel engines driving two shafts with a total of 33,600 horsepower, giving her a speed capability of over 20 knots. The crew is 21 officers and 350 enlisted; troop-carrying capacity is about 500. These ships are called *landing ship, dock* because of their docking well, which can accommodate as many as twenty-one landing craft. The helicopter deck above the docking well is for the loading and unloading of helicopters that are not carried by the LSDs, but convey troops and equipment to and from the ships. No helicopters are normally carried aboard the LSDs.

USS *Manitowoc* (LST-1180)

This ship is a member of the *Newport* class of eighteen landing ship, tank (LST) ships, consisting of LST-1179 through LST-1198. She displaces 8,400 tons, fully loaded, and has an overall length of 562 feet, a beam of 70 feet, and a rated speed of 20 knots. These are the largest and fastest LSTs built, with modern equipment and a bow ramp instead of the bow doors of previous classes of LSTs. The LST types, originally developed in World War II, revolutionized amphibious warfare with their ability to drive their flat-bottomed bows high up on a beach, drop their ramps on dry land, and off-load great numbers of tanks, trucks, and equipment of all kinds. The main load is prepacked trucks, their cargo for combat support already in place when they are driven aboard the ships. Heavy tanks and armored vehicles are also driven aboard, ready for action immediately upon landing. These ships usually off-load to a causeway rather than a beach; however, they can be beached if no pontoons or causeways are available. Their normal draft is 17 feet aft and 11 feet forward. The shallow forward draft allows for better use of their bow ramp and permits easier beaching when necessary.

USS Whidbey Island
(LSD-41)

USS Manitowoc *(LST-1180)*

The submarine rescue ship USS **Pigeon** *(ASR-21)*

12.
LOGISTICS AND SUPPORT SHIPS

It has been said that the Navy could enter a war without its logistics ships and support ships, but it couldn't keep up the fight for very long. These noncombatant ship types include the underway replenishment ships, the material-support ships, and the other auxiliaries that are vital to sustained operations of the battle force. These are the ships that replenish the stores—fuel, food, ammunition, and repair parts—that are used by the combatant ships during their operations. They also provide the craftsmen and the machinery needed to repair damaged ships and put them back in fighting trim. They may be likened to "the man behind the man behind the gun," although they are frequently so near the actual fighting that they, too, are a part of it. A traditional Navy saying is that they provide the "beans, bullets, and black oil" needed to keep the battle forces ready to fight.

There are as many types of such support ships as there are jobs to be done. Tenders carry repair parts and have workshops for various kinds of repairs. They are "mother ships" for those types of ships assigned to their care, providing all of the essentials for forward-area support. Destroyer tenders (AD), submarine tenders (AS), and repair ships (AR) are perhaps the most important mate-rial-support types; they follow the fleet and provide the "can do" of skilled technicians.

Mobile logistics ships are those that carry supplies and are capable of *underway replenishment* of the combatant ships—that is, they pass on food, ammunition, fuel, and whatever else is needed while under way in the open ocean.

Auxiliary ships are operated in today's peacetime environment by a variety of crews: (1) active-duty Navy personnel, (2) personnel of the Naval Reserve, (3) civilian crews—provided by the civil service or a contractor—under control of the Military Sealift Command. Ships under this command are designated USNS, for United States naval ship, instead of USS for United States ship. These civilian-crewed ships also have the letter T preceding their designated ship type and hull number. Examples are: USNS *Henry J. Kaiser* (TAO-187), an oiler; USNS *Mercy* (TAH-19), a hospital ship; and USNS *Stalwart* (TAGOS-1), an ocean-surveillance ship. There are many other types of auxiliaries and support ships—rescue ships, research ships, tugs, salvage ships, and other specialized types—as many as are needed to keep a fighting fleet in fighting trim.

USS *McKee* (AS-41)

A member of the three-ship *Emory S. Land* (AS-39) class of submarine tenders, the *McKee* is designed as a mother ship for the *Los Angeles* (SSN-688) class of submarine. Displacing 23,000 tons, fully loaded, she has extensive maintenance shops and repair capabilities for submarine equipment. With a length of 646 feet, a beam of 85 feet, and full-load draft of 25 feet, the *McKee* has a single steam turbine driving a single shaft at 20,000-shaft horsepower—enough power to give her a rated speed of 20 knots. She carries a crew of about 650 officers and enlisted personnel.

USS *Yellowstone* (AD-41)

The lead ship in the *Yellowstone* class of four destroyer tenders named for geographic areas of the United States, this is a 20,000-ton displacement ship that was commissioned in 1980. Length overall is 643 feet, beam is 85 feet, and draft is 23 feet. With a single steam turbine driving a single shaft with 20,000 horsepower, the *Yellowstone* is capable of speeds up to 20 knots. She carries a crew of 37 officers and over 1,300 well-trained enlisted technicians and skilled craftsmen in the ratings required for servicing destroyers and frigates. These ships serve as floating service stations for the many destroyer-type ships under their care.

USS McKee *(AS-41)*

USS *Beaufort* (ATS-2)

This is one of only three oceangoing tugs now in commission in the Navy, and is designated a salvage and rescue ship. These three ships, of the *Edenton* (ATS-1) class, are fitted with a full suite of diving and salvage equipment. Their full-load displacement is 3,200 tons; their length is 283 feet, beam is 50 feet, and draft is 15 feet. The *Beaufort* has diesels as main engines—four engines driving two shafts—delivering 6,000 horsepower. This is a powerful little ship, capable of being used as a tug when required. With a crew of 115 officers and enlisted personnel, she can handle a variety of salvage and rescue missions.

USS **Yellowstone** *(AD-41)*

USS **Beaufort** *(ATS-2)*

The USCGC **Eagle** *(WIX-327)*

13.
COAST GUARD CUTTERS

The U.S. Coast Guard classifies all of its waterborne ships and craft as *vessels;* some are called *cutters,* and others are known as *boats.* At one time the term cutter referred only to the large, speedy ships used for ocean patrols, but in recent years it has come to be the classification of all of the larger Coast Guard vessels. Even the patrol boats (WPBs) and icebreakers (WAGBs) larger than 65 feet in length are known as cutters. Those smaller than 65 feet long are called boats, or patrol boats.

These terms differ somewhat from those of the Navy; however, they are based on Coast Guard history and traditions, and are well-known and accepted terminology.

USCGC *Hamilton* (WHEC-715)

The lead ship of the *Hamilton* class of twelve high-endurance cutters—so called because they are capable of thirty to forty-five days at sea without support—the

USCGC **Hamilton** *(WHEC-715)*

Hamilton is one of nine named for Secretaries of the Treasury. Treasury is the department to which the Coast Guard was attached. The last three cutters of the class were named after heroes of the Coast Guard, hence the class is sometimes referred to as the Hero class. These vessels are the largest cutters in the Coast Guard (except the polar-class icebreakers), and the first U.S. combatant vessels to be equipped with gas turbines. In addition to two gas turbines (for high-speed power), cutters of this class have two diesel engines driving twin shafts; they can cruise on diesel power at 11 knots for some 14,000 nautical miles. When speed is important, they can light off the gas turbines and increase speed to 29 knots. These are 3,000-ton displacement vessels; their length is 378 feet, beam is 43 feet, and maximum draft is 20 feet. Armed with a 76-millimeter gun, two 20-millimeter machine guns, four 50-caliber machine guns, and six torpedo tubes, the *Hamilton* is a capable vessel with the speed, firepower, and ASW resources to hold her own in assigned wartime missions as well as in the peacetime missions of the Coast Guard. She is operated by a crew of 155 officers and enlisted men and women.

USCGC *Bear* (WMEC-901)

The *Bear* is the first of a class of thirteen cutters officially known as the Famous class, but usually referred to as the *Bear* class. She displaces about 1800 tons, full load, and is

USCGC **Bear** *(WMEC-901)*

*USCGC **Active** (WMEC-618)*

270 feet in length with a 38-foot beam and 14-foot draft. Her twin diesels driving two shafts are capable of about 20 knots maximum speed. The cutters in this class are called *medium-endurance cutters* because they are expected to be able to remain at sea for ten to thirty days without support. Normally they plan to operate at sea for twenty-one days without support, if required to do so. A multi-mission cutter, the *Bear* is well armed with one 76-millimeter gun and four 50-caliber machine guns for law enforcement and for convoy-escort duties during wartime.

USCGC *Active* (WMEC-618)

A smaller medium-endurance cutter of the *Reliance* (WMEC-615) class, the *Active* displaces 1,000 tons (full load), and is 211 feet in length. Her two turbo-charged diesels, two gas turbines, and twin shafts give her a maximum rated speed of 18 knots. Only the first five cutters of the class are equipped with gas turbines. Primarily designed for search and rescue, the *Reliance* class of sixteen cutters can land helicopters, but the ships have no hangars for them and no permanently assigned helicopters.

Artist's Concept: 120-foot WPB (Heritage class)

14.
PATROL BOATS AND ICEBREAKERS

The patrol boats of the Coast Guard are small, fast, seaworthy cutters used for search and rescue, port security, and general patrol duties. They are usually of shallow draft to facilitate operations in the inland waters of small harbors and bays. Although lightly armed, they have adequate weapons to support their law-enforcement activities. These vessels are called cutters even though their official name indicates that they are patrol boats, because of the Coast Guard custom of referring to vessels longer than 65 feet as cutters—all of the Coast Guard patrol boats in active service are longer than 65 feet.

Icebreakers are very important to the Coast Guard: they open arctic and antarctic passageways for other types of vessels, and they clear icebound harbors and seaways so that merchant ships can operate in severe cold weather. The icebreakers have long, round-bottomed, heavily constructed bows that ride up on the ice, allowing the weight of the vessel to break through and push aside the broken pieces of ice. The larger icebreakers can force a passage through heavy ice that would not yield to other types of vessels. The Coast Guard also operates an icebreaker on the Great Lakes, helping to keep vital commercial traffic flowing when the water is frozen. There are also smaller icebreaker tugs (WTGBs), known

USCGC **Metompkin** *(WPB-1325)*

as *harbor icebreakers*. In addition to regular towing services, these tugs can keep harbors and river channels navigable if ice is less than 2 feet thick. The Coast Guard has four oceangoing and eight inland-waters icebreakers in service. Two additional large (460 feet in overall length) polar icebreakers are planned as replacements for the older two icebreakers.

120-foot class of WPBs

This is a planned new class of patrol boats to be named the Heritage class. They will replace the older WPBs of several classes, some of which are over thirty years old. Replacement will begin in the early 1990s, as construction of the Heritage class begins to send these new cutters to sea. They are expected to displace about 160 tons, full load, and to have twin diesels driving two shafts. Maximum rated speed of 30 knots is one of the design goals of this new class.

USCGC *Metompkin* (WPB-1325)

The *Metompkin* is a member of the Island class of patrol boats—a class of thirty-seven cutters. Their design is primarily intended for offshore patrol and for search-and-rescue operations. They displace about 165 tons and have an overall length of 109 feet, beam of 21 feet, and draft of 7 feet. Two diesels and two shafts for propulsion allow speeds of up to 26 knots.

USCGC *Point Hannon* (WPB-82355)

There are some fifty of these 82-foot WPBs in active service, providing port security patrols and search-and-rescue missions. They are called the Point class and have seen many years of service. Two diesels and twin shafts permit speeds of about 23 knots.

USCGC *Polar Star* (WAGB-10)

One of two classes (of two ships each) of polar icebreakers in active Coast Guard service, the *Polar Star* class consists of WAGB-10 and WAGB-11. Two new polar icebreakers are planned, but except for a length overall of 460 feet, their design is not yet firm. These icebreakers will probably be replacements for the older Winds class—the *Westwind* (WAGB-281) and *Northwind* (WAGB-282)—both in service since 1945. The *Polar Star* and *Polar Sea* (WAGB-11) are 400 feet in length with an 83-foot beam and a 33-foot draft. Displacing about 13,000 tons when fully loaded, they are the largest icebreakers in the world except for those of the Soviet Union. Icebreakers require powerful propulsion systems to drive their bows high up on thick ice. The *Polar Star* class has a main-propulsion system of six diesel engines, generating some 18,000 horsepower. In addition, they have three gas turbines that can develop 60,000 horsepower for the three shafts required to drive the ships. Maximum speed is 18 knots in unobstructed water; in

USCGC Point Hannon
(WPB 82355)

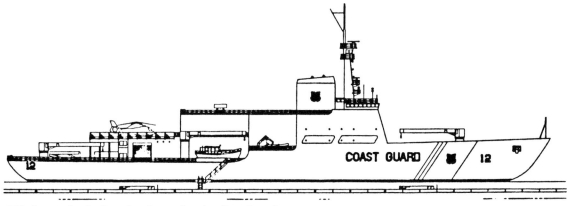

460-foot polar icebreaker (new class)—line drawing

USCGC **Polar Star** *(WAGB-10)*

ice-covered water it is considerably slower. These ships also carry two helicopters to assist in searching out the most promising paths through heavy ice. The *Polar Sea* was the first ship ever to circle North America. She traveled through the Panama Canal, the Northwest Passage, and the Bering Sea in about four months to accomplish this feat.

USCGC *Mobile Bay* (WTGB-103)

The *Mobile Bay* is one of ten of the Bay class of large tugs that can also be used to break through ice of up to two feet in thickness. Like all tugs, they are powerful vessels; diesel-electric drives of 2,500 horsepower give them the ability to make 15 knots maximum speed and to tow much larger vessels when necessary. These cutters have an overall length of 140 feet, a beam of 37 feet, and a maximum full-load draft of 12 feet. They have a full-load displacement of about 650 tons.

USCGC **Mobile Bay** *(WTGB-103)*

Artist's Concept: The **Ticonderoga** *and* **Arleigh Burke**

15.
ADVANCED SHIP DESIGNS

Ship designs change as the years go by. The U.S. Navy and Coast Guard are constantly looking ahead, seeking newer and better technologies, and designing new ships and boats that will perform future missions more effectively. The objective of new designs is to replace older, obsolete ships and to increase the readiness and effectiveness of our sea services.

Some new Navy types are the result of changes in the technology and techniques of warfare—the guided-missile ships and the nuclear-powered ships, for example. In earlier years the progress being made in aviation led to ships that were intended to be "carriers of aeroplanes" or "floating aerodromes." As a result of the successful use of aircraft in warfare at sea, today's Navy is strongly oriented toward aircraft carriers and their modern warplanes.

Certain new types result from changes in mission. The fleet ballistic missile submarine developed from the need for the Navy to assume the new role of preventing enemy attacks. Thus a new mission—strategic deterrence—resulted in perfection of a new type of ship, the SSBN.

The Coast Guard rescue mission, at times requiring the service to provide assistance to ships in remote areas, calls for cutters with the ability to enter northern areas where large sections of the ocean surface may be covered with a thick sheet of ice. These mission requirements made necessary the development of vessels especially designed for breaking through heavy ice; thus icebreakers became a new and specialized type of Coast Guard vessel.

Ships of the future for both the Navy and the Coast Guard will, in most cases, result from advances in the technology of ship design and construction. As technological improvements are made in forms of propulsion (electric drive, superconductivity, supercavitating propellers, water-jet propulsion) and in hull forms (SWATH, SES, Seaknife, hydrofoil), plans for new vessels will change accordingly.

Today there is great emphasis placed on entirely new forms of ships. Test programs have shown that specialized types may have certain advantages attractive to both the Navy and Coast Guard. All new proposals and concepts, no matter how extreme, are given consideration. They are studied carefully, since some may represent breakthrough designs. It is never certain that new concepts will survive the years until a ship is approved for construction; any concept may also become outdated because of later improvements. One can visualize the Navy and Coast Guard of the future by observing some of the new ship and

COAST GUARD

1001

1001

COASTAL SURVEILLANCE CUTTER
(WSEC-1001)

Artist's Concept: SWATH coastal surveillance cutter

Artist's Concept: SWATH ship for ocean research (Courtesy Blue Sea Corporation/Key Ocean Services, Inc.)

boat designs now under consideration. Some of these may be illustrated, as shown in this section. Many of the new ships will never be built—they are only conceptual, and represent only tentative ideas. Some will be built, and others are already under construction. Many of the ideas are for the distant future, since it takes a long time to go from the conceptual stage to a commissioned ship. A few of the new design concepts now being studied are described on the following pages. Some advanced designs that have reached the testing and early operational stages are also presented.

Small waterplane area, twin hull (SWATH) ship

SWATH is an acronym for small waterplane area twin hull, which simply means that most of the ship's hull is submerged in the calm water that lies below the disturbed ocean surface, with only small columns (waterplane areas) projecting through the surface to support the upper hull. A SWATH ship resembles a broad platform on streamlined stilts, or in some cases on long, narrow, single struts that connect the upper hull to the two submerged lower hulls. The SWATH design permits great steadiness in rough seas, allowing for conduct of operations that require a stable platform. An important asset of this design is that it permits large deck areas, since the twin hulls are usually placed far enough apart to give excellent stability. The Navy is using the SWATH concept for some of its ocean surveillance ships (auxiliary general ocean surveillance—AGOS) to provide better seakeeping and allow for improved operations in stormy areas. Even though the SWATH is essentially a low-speed ship, it has been suggested as an option for small aircraft carriers, possibly to operate short takeoff and landing STOL/VSTOL aircraft. The inherent SWATH characteristics—a very stable platform with large deck area—make small SWATH carriers an attractive possibility for future Navy use. The Coast Guard may find these ships helpful in rescue operations during storms or for buoy tenders, where a stable platform is a great asset when positioning or recovering buoys.

Artist's Concept: SWATH ship carrier for STOL/VSTOL aircraft

Surface effect ship (SES)

Surface effect ships benefit from the near-surface lift provided by a layer of pressurized air held in a space beneath the ship's specially designed hull. They are capable of great speeds, as high as 80 knots. These ships ride on an air bubble contained by catamaran-like sidewalls and flexible, rubber curtains (called *skirts*) at the bow and stern. They maintain the bubble with large propellers or gas turbines blowing air into the cavity under the hull. This pressure is sufficient to raise most of the ship above the surface, leaving only the lower parts of the sidewalls and flexible skirts penetrating the surface and holding the air bubble. With the decreased drag associated with being "up on the bubble," these ships can make greater speeds than ships with large submerged hulls. The SES design has been suggested as a revolutionary warship that could race across oceans at speeds of 80

Artist's Concept: Large surface effect ship

knots or higher. A number of small experimental craft have been built and tested by the Navy and Coast Guard; one of them, which displaces 200 tons, has been designated as WSES-1 by the Coast Guard. Among future designs suggested for the Navy is a prototype SES warship of about 3,000 tons displacement, 275 feet long, with a 105-foot beam. This ship would be powered by six gas turbines.

Air cushion vehicles (ACV)

These are somewhat like the SES design, but they differ in that they have flexible seals all around and no sidewalls. One advantage to having rubber seals instead of rigid sidewalls is that as the ACV hull rides high above the water, only the bottom tips of the seals touch the surface. Thus the ACV is able to move over shallow water or mud flats, land surfaces, beach areas, and concrete ramps. Extensive use on land, however, can cause rapid wear of the rubber seals, requiring frequent replacement. Nevertheless, the ability to cross very shallow water areas and solid ground is an important asset when making amphibious landings. One type of ACV, the LCAC (amphibious craft, air cushion) is in active Navy service. About ninety of these, each of which weighs 200 tons when fully loaded, are planned. They are powered by four gas turbines—two for propulsion, two for lift. Their top speed over relatively calm water is approximately 50 knots.

Six PHMs foilborne at 40 knots

Coast Guard test hydrofoil

Hydrofoil ship

The hydrofoil uses a traditional warship hull equipped with three *foils,* or winglike appendages that can be lowered beneath the ship. As speed builds up, the foils create lift and elevate the hull above the ocean surface, leaving only the foils in the water. The hydrofoil ships are then said to be *flying on their foils.* By thus decreasing the drag of the hull, this design allows for greatly improved speed. In addition, by elevating the hull above the waves, high-speed operation in rough seas is possible. The Navy now has six missile-firing hydrofoils in active service: the *Pegasus* (PHM-1) class. All of the ships are assisting in the interdiction of drug smugglers. The *Pegasus* displaces about 250 tons, full load, and is powered by two diesel engines and one gas turbine. With water-jet propulsion, when foil-borne she can make about 50 knots. If the design can be successfully adapted to larger ships, hydrofoils may be used more extensively by both the Navy and the Coast Guard.

Artist's Concept: Cutaway view of missile ship
(Drawing by Tom Freeman)

Missile carrier ship

The concept of a single ship type to transport, maintain, and launch a variety of missiles is an interesting possibility. Such a ship could launch missiles on command from other ships of the battle group, with the requesting ship then taking over the control and target-designation functions. The missile ships would be able to store large quantities of all types of missiles, thus relieving other ship types of the need to maintain an inventory and replenish it frequently in battle areas. In effect, the missile ship would be a combination storehouse and launch platform for the entire battle group. When missile supplies were exhausted, it would be replaced by another, fully stocked, missile ship and would return to port for reloading.

INDEX

The Naval Institute Press is part of the U.S. Naval Institute, an organization for sea service professionals and civilians with an interest in the navies of the world. Established in 1873 at the U.S. Naval Academy in Annapolis, Maryland, where its offices remain today, the Naval Institute has more than 100,000 members.

Members of the Naval Institute receive the influential monthly naval magazine *Proceedings* and discounts on fine nautical prints, ship and aircraft photos, and subscriptions to the quarterly *Naval History* magazine. They also have access to the transcripts of the Institute's Oral History Program and get discounted admission to the Institute-sponsored seminars offered around the country.

The Naval Institute's book-publishing program, begun in 1898 with basic guides to naval practices, has broadened its scope in recent years to include books of more general interest. Now the Naval Institute Press publishes more than forty new titles each year, ranging from how-to books on boating and navigation to battle histories, biographies, ship and aircraft guides, and novels. Members receive discounts on the Press's more than 350 books.

Full-time students are eligible for special half-price membership rates. Life memberships are also available.

For a free catalog describing the Naval Institute Press books currently available and for further information about U.S. Naval Institute membership, please write to:

Membership & Communications Department
U.S. Naval Institute
Annapolis, Maryland 21402

or call, toll-free, (800) 233-USNI. In Maryland call (301) 268-6110.

Rear Admiral M. D. Van Orden, USN (Ret.), graduated from the U.S. Naval Academy in 1944 and served in the Pacific until the end of World War II, earning four battle stars on his Asiatic-Pacific Campaign Medal, a Victory Medal, a Philippine Liberation Medal, and other decorations. He was twice awarded the Legion of Merit Medal. During his thirty-four-year naval career, he served in a variety of ships, including a battleship, an aircraft carrier, a minesweeper, and an attack transport. He later managed the research, development, and acquisition of naval electronic systems. At the time of his retirement in 1975 he was chief of naval research, having directed the navy's $300 million research program for two years.

In addition to earning his degree from the Naval Academy, Admiral Van Orden won degrees from the Massachusetts Institute of Technology and George Washington University. He now lives in McLean, Virginia, where he works as a senior management analyst for a private company and as the chief executive officer for the Surgical Rehabilitation Foundation.